Build Your Own AI: A Beginner's Guide to Running Local AI Models with LM Studio & DeepSeek

Install, Customize, and Optimize AI Offline Using Local Data—No Cloud Required!

Table of Contents

1. Introduction to Local AI

- Why Run AI Locally? (Privacy, Performance, Cost)
- What You'll Learn in This Book
- Understanding LM Studio and DeepSeek

2. Setting Up Your AI Environment

- System Requirements & Recommended Hardware
- Installing LM Studio on Windows, Mac, and Linux

- Configuring LM Studio for Best Performance

3. Downloading & Running DeepSeek Models

- Understanding DeepSeek: What It Is and How It Works
- Finding the Right Model: GPT-style, Coding Assistants, and More
- Downloading & Installing DeepSeek AI Models

4. Using Local AI Models Efficiently

- Basic Commands & Interactions
- Running AI Locally Without Internet Access
- Optimizing Response Time and Accuracy

5. Training & Fine-Tuning AI with Local Data

- Why Train AI on Local Data?
- Preparing & Formatting Your Data
- Training Basics: Using Your Own Files for Custom AI Responses

6. Advanced Customization & Optimization

- Adjusting Model Parameters for Better Results
- Using External Tools to Enhance Local AI Performance
- Troubleshooting Common Issues (Slow Response, High CPU Usage, etc.)

7. Real-World Applications of Local AI

- Creating a Personal AI Assistant
- Using AI for Content Creation & Research
- Automating Repetitive Tasks with AI

8. Future of Local AI & Next Steps

- Upcoming AI Trends & Improvements
- How to Stay Updated with AI Advancements
- Resources for Further Learning

CONCLUSION

Build Your Own AI: A Beginner's Guide to Running Local AI Models with LM Studio & DeepSeek

Install, Customize, and Optimize AI Offline Using Local Data—No Cloud Required!

CHAPTER 1: Introduction to Local AI

Why Run AI Locally? (Privacy, Performance, Cost)

Artificial intelligence (AI) is transforming the way we work, create, and interact with technology. However, most AI applications rely on cloud-based services that come with privacy risks, performance limitations, and recurring costs. Running AI models locally offers several advantages:

- **Privacy & Security** – Your data stays on your machine, reducing exposure to third-party servers.
- **Performance & Speed** – No network latency means faster processing and real-time responses.
- **Cost Efficiency** – Avoid ongoing subscription fees and API usage costs.
- **Customization & Control** – Run AI models tailored to your needs without platform restrictions.

This book will guide you through setting up your local AI environment, ensuring you maximize these benefits.

What You'll Learn in This Book

This book is a step-by-step guide to running AI models locally, specifically focusing on **LM Studio** and **DeepSeek**. By the end of this guide, you will have a fully functional AI setup running on your computer, capable of handling various natural language processing tasks without internet dependency. You will learn:

- How to install **LM Studio** and configure it for optimal performance.
- Where to download **DeepSeek**, a powerful open-source AI model.
- How to use **local data** to fine-tune AI for personal or business applications.
- Best practices for optimizing your AI workflow without cloud reliance.

Understanding LM Studio and DeepSeek

Before diving into installation and usage, it's essential to understand the two core tools we'll be working with:

- **LM Studio**: A user-friendly platform for managing and running large language models (LLMs) locally on your machine. It simplifie model downloads, configuration, and interaction.
- **DeepSeek**: A state-of-the-art AI model designed for efficiency, accuracy, and offline use. It is one of the best open-source alternatives to cloud-based AI services like OpenAI's GPT.

By leveraging **LM Studio** and **DeepSeek**, you can unlock the power of AI on your own terms—without sharing sensitive data or relying on costly cloud services.

CHAPTER 2: Setting Up Your AI Environment

System Requirements & Recommended Hardware

Before installing LM Studio, ensure your system meets the necessary requirements for optimal performance. Running AI models locally requires significant computational power, particularly for larger models. Below are the recommended hardware specifications:

Minimum Requirements:

- **CPU:** Intel Core i5 (10th Gen) / AMD Ryzen 5 (3000 series) or equivalent
- **RAM:** 8GB
- **GPU:** Integrated graphics (not recommended for larger models)
- **Storage:** 20GB free space (SSD preferred)
- **OS:** Windows 10/11, macOS 12+, or Linux (Ubuntu 20.04+)

Recommended Requirements:

- **CPU:** Intel Core i7 (12th Gen) / AMD Ryzen 7 (5000 series) or higher
- **RAM:** 32GB+
- **GPU:** NVIDIA RTX 3060 (12GB VRAM) / AMD Radeon RX 6800 or higher
- **Storage:** 100GB free space (NVMe SSD for best performance)
- **OS:** Windows 11, macOS 13+, or latest Linux distributions

Installing LM Studio on Windows, Mac, and Linux

Windows Installation:

1. **Download LM Studio** from the official website.
2. **Run the installer** and follow on-screen instructions.
3. Choose the **installation directory** (default is usually fine).
4. Allow the installer to complete and **restart your system** if prompted.

5. Open LM Studio and verify the installation by running a test model.

Mac Installation:

1. **Download LM Studio** (macOS version) from the official source.
2. Open the **.dmg file** and drag LM Studio to the Applications folder.
3. Open LM Studio; if you receive a security prompt, allow it under **System Preferences > Security & Privacy**.
4. Verify the installation by running a test model.

Linux Installation:

1. Open a terminal and install necessary dependencies:
2. sudo apt update && sudo apt install -y build-essential
3. Download the LM Studio Linux package from the official source.
4. Extract the package and navigate to the installation directory:

5. tar -xvf lmstudio-linux.tar.gz

6. cd lmstudio-linux

7. Run the installation script:

8. ./install.sh

9. Launch LM Studio and verify the setup.

Configuring LM Studio for Best Performance

Once LM Studio is installed, configuring it properly ensures smooth and efficient AI model execution.

1. Allocating GPU Resources:

- Open LM Studio settings and enable **GPU acceleration** if available.
- Adjust memory allocation based on your GPU's VRAM.

2. Optimizing Model Performance:

- Use **quantized models (e.g., 4-bit or 8-bit)** to reduce RAM and VRAM usage.
- Close background applications to free system resources.

3. Adjusting CPU & RAM Usage :

- If using CPU mode, increase **thread count** to leverage multi-core processors.
- Increase swap space on Linux if RAM is limited:
- sudo fallocate -l 16G /swapfile
- sudo chmod 600 /swapfile
- sudo mkswap /swapfile
- sudo swapon /swapfile

4. Enabling Offline Mode:

- Download models in advance to run offline.
- Ensure LM Studio is set to **local processing** mode.

By following these steps, you will have a properly configured AI environment ready for local processing and experimentation.

Chapter 3: Downloading & Running DeepSeek Models

Understanding DeepSeek: What It Is and How It Works

DeepSeek is a powerful AI model designed to assist with various tasks, including natural language processing (NLP), coding, and general AI applications. It is similar to OpenAI's GPT models but can be run locally, providing privacy and customization advantages. DeepSeek offers different versions optimized for tasks such as text generation, code completion, and chatbot functionalities.

The key benefits of using DeepSeek include:

- **Offline Usage:** No internet connection required after installation.
- **Customization:** Ability to fine-tune and use local datasets.
- **Privacy Control:** No data is sent to external servers.

DeepSeek models are available in different sizes and capabilities, allowing users to select one based on their hardware and use case.

Finding the Right Model: GPT-Style, Coding Assistants, and More

DeepSeek offers a variety of AI models catering to different needs. Here are the primary categories:

1. **DeepSeek GPT** – A general-purpose AI model similar to ChatGPT, useful for text generation, summarization, and Q&A.
2. **DeepSeek Code** – Designed specifically for code completion and programming assistance.
3. **Fine-Tuned Variants** – Some models are fine-tuned for specific applications, such as legal, medical, or creative writing tasks.

Choosing the Right Model Size

DeepSeek models come in different parameter sizes (e.g., 7B, 13B, 67B). The choice depends on your hardware:

- **Low-End Systems (8GB RAM, no GPU):** Smaller models like 7B are recommended.

- **Mid-Range Systems (16GB RAM, basic GPU):** Can run 13B models with reasonable performance.

- **High-End Systems (32GB+ RAM, powerful GPU):** Can run large models (67B) for high-quality results.

Downloading & Installing DeepSeek AI Models

To run DeepSeek models locally, you need to download and install them properly. Follow these steps:

Step 1: Install LM Studio

LM Studio is a user-friendly tool for managing local AI models. It simplifies the process of downloading, configuring, and running models.

1. Download LM Studio from its official website.
2. Install it on your system following the on-screen instructions.

Step 2: Download the DeepSeek Model

1. Open LM Studio and navigate to the model library.
2. Search for "DeepSeek" in the available models.
3. Select the appropriate model version based on your system's specifications.
4. Click "Download" and wait for the process to complete.

Step 3: Configure and Run the Model

1. Load the model in LM Studio.
2. Adjust settings such as:
   - **Memory allocation**
   - **GPU acceleration (if available)**
   - **Inference parameters (temperature, max tokens, etc.)**
3. Start the model and test responses in the built-in chat interface.

Troubleshooting Common Issues

- **Model Not Loading?** Ensure your system meets the minimum RAM and VRAM requirements.

- **Slow Response Time?** Reduce model size or adjust performance settings.

- **Errors on Startup?** Check installation paths and dependencies.

By following these steps, you can successfully download and run DeepSeek AI models on your local machine, enabling powerful AI applications without relying on cloud-based services.

Chapter 4: Using Local AI Models Efficiently

Basic Commands & Interactions

Once you have installed LM Studio and downloaded DeepSeek, you need to understand the basic commands for interacting with your local AI model. Below are some fundamental commands to get started:

Launching the AI Model

lmstudio start --model deepseek

This command initiates the AI model and prepares it for interactions.

Sending Queries to the Model

You can interact with your AI model via the command line or a script. For example:

from lmstudio import AIModel

model = AIModel("deepseek")

```
response = model.query("What is the capital of
France?")
print(response)
```

This script initializes the AI model and queries it for information.

Adjusting Model Parameters

You can tweak the AI model for better performance by adjusting parameters such as:

```
lmstudio start --model deepseek --temperature
0.7 --max_tokens 500
```

- temperature: Controls the randomness of responses (lower values make it more deterministic).
- max_tokens: Limits the response length to ensure efficiency.

Running AI Locally Without Internet Access

One of the key benefits of using local AI models is that they function offline. To ensure smooth operation:

1. **Disable Internet Access**: If you want to confirm that your AI is truly running offline, disable your network connection and test it.
2. **Preload Required Data**: Ensure any datasets or knowledge sources your AI model requires are pre-downloaded.
3. **Use Local APIs**: When building applications, point them to local APIs rather than web-based endpoints. Example:

```
model = AIModel("deepseek", local=True)
```

This ensures all processing happens on your machine without external connections.

Optimizing Response Time and Accuracy

To maximize performance and efficiency, consider the following:

Optimize System Resources

- Close unnecessary applications to free up CPU and RAM.
- Allocate more resources to LM Studio if possible.
- Use GPU acceleration if your hardware supports it.

Reduce Latency

- Use a smaller model variant if response time is slow.
- Pre-load frequently used queries into memory.

Fine-Tune for Accuracy

- Train the model on your specific dataset for better relevance.

- Adjust hyperparameters such as temperature and top_p to balance creativity and precision.

By following these techniques, you can run AI models locally with efficiency, ensuring both speed and accuracy without relying on the internet.

CHAPTER 5. Training & Fine-Tuning AI with Local Data

Why Train AI on Local Data?

Training AI on local data has several benefits. By using your own data, you can create a highly customized AI model that understands your specific use case, industry, or personal preferences. Here are a few key reasons to use local data:

1. **Tailored Responses**: The AI will be able to generate responses that are more relevant to your needs, as it is trained on your own data.
2. **Improved Accuracy**: With access to local knowledge, the AI can provide more accurate and contextually appropriate answers.
3. **Privacy & Security**: Using your own data means you're not relying on external datasets, reducing the risk of privacy concerns or data breaches.

4. **Control Over Training**: You have full control over the data used for training, enabling you to avoid unwanted biases and noise from third-party datasets.

Preparing & Formatting Your Data

Before you can train AI on your local data, it's crucial to prepare it in the correct format. AI models need structured input data to make sense of it and learn from it effectively. Here's how to prepare your data:

1. **Organize Your Data**: Gather and categorize your data. For example, if you are training a model for customer service, you may want to collect FAQs, customer interactions, or product descriptions.

2. **Data Formatting**: Convert your data into machine-readable formats such as CSV, JSON, or text files. Ensure consistency in data formatting for best results.

3. **Clean Your Data**: Remove irrelevant or duplicate entries and fix any

inconsistencies to improve the quality of your dataset.

4. **Data Annotation**: For supervised learning, label your data with the right categories or outcomes to guide the AI's learning process. This is especially important for tasks like sentiment analysis or classification.

Training Basics: Using Your Own Files for Custom AI Responses

Once your data is ready, it's time to start training the AI model. Here's an overview of the process:

1. **Set Up the Training Environment**: Before you begin, make sure you have a working setup of tools like LM Studio or any other software that allows you to train AI locally.

2. **Choose the Model Architecture**: Decide on the architecture that best suits your needs. For example, if you're working with text data, you may choose models like GPT or BERT.

3. **Upload Your Data**: Load your cleaned and formatted data into the training tool. Most

training tools allow you to upload files directly, so the data is fed into the model.

4. **Train the Model**: With your data uploaded, you can initiate the training process. Depending on the size of your dataset and model complexity, training could take some time. You may need to adjust training parameters such as learning rate, batch size, and number of epochs to optimize the process.

5. **Monitor Training Progress**: Keep an eye on the model's performance during training. Use tools like loss graphs and accuracy metrics to track the AI's progress.

6. **Fine-Tuning**: After training the base model, fine-tune it using specific datasets that are most relevant to your use case. This helps the AI become more adept at handling the tasks you care about.

7. **Test and Evaluate**: After training, test the model with unseen data to evaluate its performance. Adjust the model if necessary and retrain with more data to further improve its responses.

CHAPTER 6: Advanced Customization & Optimization

Adjusting Model Parameters for Better Results

To get the best performance from your AI model, you may need to fine-tune various parameters. Here's how you can adjust settings to improve the AI's responses:

1. **Learning Rate**: This determines how quickly the model adapts during training. A higher learning rate can speed up learning but might cause instability, while a lower rate ensures more stable learning but might take longer.

2. **Batch Size**: The batch size controls how many data points are used in one iteration of training. Larger batch sizes can speed up training but require more memory. Smaller batches can result in more precise learning, though they may take longer.

3. **Epochs**: The number of epochs defines how many times the model will iterate over the entire training dataset. More epochs can

lead to better training, but it also risks overfitting if the model learns the training data too well.

4. **Dropout Rate**: This is used to prevent overfitting by randomly "dropping" units during training. Experimenting with the dropout rate helps to strike a balance between underfitting and overfitting.

5. **Optimization Algorithms**: Different optimization algorithms like Adam, SGD (Stochastic Gradient Descent), and RMSprop affect how the model updates its weights. Depending on your task, experimenting with different optimizers can yield better results.

6. **Regularization**: Methods like L2 regularization or early stopping can help your model generalize better on unseen data, improving its accuracy and robustness.

Experiment with these parameters and run multiple training sessions to see which combinations work best for your data and specific application.

Using External Tools to Enhance Local AI Performance

While your AI model may be trained locally, you can enhance its performance using external tools and resources. These can boost efficiency, provide additional functionality, or integrate with other systems:

1. **Data Augmentation Tools**: Using external tools like text augmentation libraries or image generation tools can help you expand your training data. This is especially useful for tasks like natural language processing (NLP) or computer vision, where large datasets improve model accuracy.

2. **Pre-trained Models**: Instead of starting from scratch, you can leverage pre-trained models available in public repositories like Hugging Face, TensorFlow Hub, or other open-source AI platforms. You can fine-tune these models with your local data to

achieve better performance with less training time.

3. **Cloud Resources**: Although your AI is running locally, occasional cloud support (for computational heavy-lifting) can help speed up training or inference times. Services like Google Colab or AWS offer on-demand GPU power for faster training.

4. **External APIs for Enrichment**: Integrate your AI model with APIs that offer additional insights or data sources, such as sentiment analysis, translations, or knowledge graphs. This can make your model more powerful and dynamic.

5. **Performance Monitoring Tools**: Tools like TensorBoard or Weights & Biases allow you to monitor your model's performance over time, compare different training runs, and track metrics such as accuracy, loss, and training speed.

Troubleshooting Common Issues (Slow Response, High CPU Usage, etc.)

During training or when using a locally deployed AI model, you might face performance issues. Here are common problems and solutions:

1. **Slow Response Times**:
   - **Large Model Size**: Large AI models may take longer to generate responses. You can reduce the model size by using quantization techniques or pruning irrelevant weights.
   - **Optimization**: Ensure that your model's inference pipeline is optimized. Try using batch processing for multiple queries or offload non-essential computations to a separate thread or process.
   - **Caching**: Implement caching strategies where previously computed responses or computations are stored to avoid repeating expensive calculations.

2. **High CPU Usage**:
   - ○ **Overloaded Model**: If the model is too large for your hardware, consider using a lighter model or reducing the complexity of the model.
   - ○ **Parallel Processing**: Distribute computations across multiple cores or use specialized hardware like GPUs or TPUs if available to offload processing tasks.
   - ○ **Memory Leaks**: Check if there are any memory leaks in the code. Ensure that unnecessary variables and data are freed up after use.
   - ○ **Batch Processing**: Process data in smaller batches to reduce the strain on your CPU.
3. **Overfitting**:
   - ○ **Regularization**: Use techniques like dropout or L2 regularization to prevent your model from memorizing the training data.
   - ○ **Cross-validation**: Use cross-validation to evaluate how well your

model generalizes to unseen data and adjust training parameters accordingly.

4. **Underfitting**:
   - ○ **Model Complexity**: If your model is too simple, it might not capture the complexity of your data. Try increasing the model's layers or using more advanced architectures.
   - ○ **Data Issues**: Make sure your training data is comprehensive and representative of the real-world scenarios the model will encounter. More diverse data can help improve the model's ability to generalize.

5. **Unexpected Outputs**:
   - ○ **Data Quality**: Poor-quality data can lead to the model producing unexpected or biased outputs. Double-check your data preprocessing and cleaning steps.
   - ○ **Parameter Tuning**: Adjust hyperparameters such as learning

rate, batch size, or optimizer choice if the model is not converging properly.

By following these tips, you can ensure that your AI model remains efficient, scalable, and responsive even as you make it more advanced and tailored to your specific use case.

CHAPTER 7: Real-World Applications of Local AI

Creating a Personal AI Assistant

A personal AI assistant can be customized to meet your specific needs, whether it's for personal productivity, managing tasks, or helping you make informed decisions. Here's how to create one using local AI:

1. **Define the Scope**: Decide what tasks you want your AI assistant to handle. Common applications include:
   - Scheduling and calendar management
   - Email or message handling
   - Data analysis and reporting
   - Task reminders and to-do lists
2. **Design the Conversation Flow**: Based on your needs, create a conversation flow for your AI assistant. You can customize the responses it gives for specific tasks, questions, or triggers, using your trained

model to ensure the assistant fits your personality or style.

3. **Integrating APIs**: You can enhance the assistant by connecting it to external APIs for additional functionalities, such as weather updates, news, or even managing smart devices at home.

4. **Voice Capabilities**: If you want your assistant to support voice commands, you can use speech recognition tools like Google Speech API or offline voice processing libraries to integrate voice recognition and response.

5. **Local Data Integration**: Make your assistant even more personalized by having it access and use local files, emails, notes, and other relevant documents to deliver responses and suggestions tailored specifically to you.

6. **Privacy Considerations**: Since everything is running locally, your assistant will only use data stored on your device, ensuring maximum privacy and control over your personal information.

Using AI for Content Creation & Research

AI can be a powerful tool for content creators and researchers. Here's how you can use local AI for generating content and conducting research:

1. **Content Generation**: Whether it's for blog posts, articles, or even books, you can use your trained AI to generate text that fits specific topics or styles. Fine-tuning the model on your preferred writing style or target audience can yield more personalized content.

2. **Summarizing Information**: AI can help you digest large amounts of text by summarizing articles, papers, or reports into concise summaries, making research more efficient.

3. **Topic Ideation**: AI can help generate ideas for content by analyzing trends or suggesting related topics based on your niche. It can also assist in identifying gaps in existing content that you can target with fresh ideas.

4. **Keyword Analysis**: For SEO purposes, AI models can be trained to help identify trending keywords, suggest improvements, or analyze how your content ranks compared to competitors' in real-time.

5. **Research Assistance**: Your AI can help you gather research data from a variety of sources, offering insights into what's being said in the academic or industry-related fields. It can analyze published papers, books, or articles to give you a detailed understanding of a subject matter.

Automating Repetitive Tasks with AI

AI can be a game-changer when it comes to automating time-consuming, repetitive tasks. Here are some examples of how to use local AI for automation:

1. **Data Entry and Management**: If you have large amounts of structured data (like customer records, inventory logs, or financial data), you can create an AI that automatically populates spreadsheets,

databases, or forms, reducing human error and saving time.

2. **Email Management**: Train your AI to automatically sort and categorize emails, flagging important ones or even drafting responses to common inquiries. It can help you stay on top of your inbox and improve response times.

3. **Social Media Management**: AI can help you manage your social media accounts by posting content, scheduling posts, and even engaging with followers using predefined templates or responses.

4. **Customer Support Automation**: Set up a chatbot or virtual assistant to answer common customer queries on your website or app. The AI can handle a wide range of inquiries without human intervention, improving customer satisfaction and reducing response times.

5. **File Management**: AI can help automate the organization of files, like categorizing documents based on their content,

renaming files for better organization, and even backing up files regularly.

6. **Automating Reports**: For business owners or analysts, AI can be trained to generate reports based on data inputs, whether it's sales reports, financial summaries, or performance tracking.

7. **Task Scheduling**: Create AI models to assist in scheduling meetings, managing appointments, or even automating reminders for deadlines or events.

By implementing AI for these tasks, you free up valuable time, allowing you to focus on more strategic or creative work.

CHAPTER 8: Future of Local AI & Next Steps

Upcoming AI Trends & Improvements

AI is evolving rapidly, and there are several key trends and improvements to watch for in the coming years, especially for locally trained models:

1. **Smarter & More Specialized Models**: As AI continues to advance, we will see more specialized models that are better at handling niche tasks. These models will be tailored for specific industries, such as healthcare, education, or legal fields, providing even more accuracy and efficiency.

2. **Improved Fine-Tuning Techniques**: The process of fine-tuning models on specific datasets will become even more refined, making it easier to customize AI models. New algorithms and techniques will allow for faster, more effective fine-tuning with less data.

3. **Edge AI**: Local AI models will be increasingly deployed on edge devices (smartphones, IoT devices, etc.), enabling faster processing and more efficient use of resources. This means AI will work directly on devices, reducing reliance on cloud servers and improving privacy.

4. **Explainability & Transparency**: The push for explainable AI is gaining momentum. More focus will be placed on making AI decisions transparent, so users can understand why a model makes certain predictions, improving trust and usability.

5. **Federated Learning**: Federated learning is a method where AI models can be trained across decentralized devices without sharing raw data. This will enhance privacy and reduce data transfer costs while still allowing for robust, distributed learning.

6. **AI-Powered Personalization**: AI will become even more personalized, learning from individual user preferences and behaviors. Expect models to understand and adapt to your unique needs more

seamlessly, from personal assistants to content recommendations.

7. **Zero-Shot & Few-Shot Learning**: AI models will continue to improve in learning with very few examples. This means you'll be able to train models with less data and still achieve high-quality results.

8. **Ethical AI & Bias Mitigation**: Efforts will continue to refine AI models to minimize bias and make ethical considerations a priority. Expect improved fairness and accountability in AI systems, especially with more localized and customized implementations.

How to Stay Updated with AI Advancements

Staying current with the fast-paced world of AI is crucial to leveraging the latest tools, techniques, and best practices. Here are some ways to stay updated:

1. **Follow Industry Leaders & AI Communities**: Follow thought leaders and researchers in the AI space on social media

platforms like Twitter, LinkedIn, and Medium. Joining online communities like Reddit's r/MachineLearning or the AI section of Stack Overflow can help you stay informed.

2. **AI Conferences & Webinars**: Attend AI-focused conferences, webinars, and workshops to hear directly from experts about the latest trends and breakthroughs. Some prominent events include NeurIPS, ICML, and CVPR.

3. **Academic Journals & Publications**: Keep up with recent research by reading academic papers and journals. Websites like ArXiv provide open-access papers on the latest AI advancements in various fields.

4. **Newsletters & Blogs**: Subscribe to AI-focused newsletters and blogs. Some popular ones include:
   - **The Batch by Andrew Ng** (Coursera)
   - **Distill.pub** for in-depth AI explanations
   - **The AI Alignment Newsletter** for ethical discussions around AI

5. **Online Courses & Platforms**: Continuously update your skills by enrolling in AI courses from platforms like Coursera, edX, or Udemy. Many of these platforms offer courses on the latest AI technologies and practices.

6. **Open-Source AI Projects**: Contribute to or follow open-source AI projects on GitHub. Open-source communities often lead the way in new advancements and can offer insight into real-world applications of cutting-edge technology.

7. **AI Research Blogs**: Subscribe to AI research blogs from institutions like OpenAI, DeepMind, and Google AI, where they post their latest findings and technical papers.

8. **AI Podcasts & Videos**: Podcasts and YouTube channels like "AI Alignment Podcast" or "Lex Fridman Podcast" often feature conversations with AI experts, keeping you updated on the most current developments.

Resources for Further Learning

If you're looking to dive deeper into AI, here are some great resources for further learning:

1. **Books**:
   - *"Deep Learning"* by Ian Goodfellow, Yoshua Bengio, and Aaron Courville
   - *"Hands-On Machine Learning with Scikit-Learn, Keras, and TensorFlow"* by Aurélien Géron
   - *"AI Superpowers"* by Kai-Fu Lee for insights into the global AI landscape.
2. **Online Courses**:
   - **Fast.ai** offers free courses on practical deep learning.
   - **Coursera's Machine Learning Specialization** by Andrew Ng.
   - **DeepLearning.AI** offers more specialized AI courses, including courses on NLP and computer vision.
3. **AI Tools & Frameworks**:
   - **TensorFlow** and **PyTorch** are two of the most popular machine learning

frameworks, offering detailed documentation and tutorials for developers.

- o **Hugging Face** provides an amazing library for NLP models and a large community of developers sharing their fine-tuned models.

4. **Research Platforms**:

- o **Google Scholar**: A powerful resource for finding academic papers on AI topics.

- o **Papers with Code**: A great platform to explore the latest AI papers and their associated code implementations.

5. **Community & Forums**:

- o **Kaggle**: Participate in machine learning competitions and learn from others' code and solutions.

- o **Stack Overflow**: A community-driven Q&A platform that's great for solving programming-related issues.

- **GitHub**: Explore the latest open-source AI projects and collaborate with others.

Conclusion

Congratulations on completing your journey through creating and working with local AI! You've learned everything from setting up your AI environment to training your models with local data, fine-tuning parameters, and deploying real-world applications. The possibilities are endless when you have the power of AI working locally, tailored to your specific needs and goals.

As AI continues to evolve, staying updated and adapting to the latest advancements will be key to unlocking even greater potential. Whether you're building personal assistants, automating tasks, or exploring new frontiers in content creation and research, you're now equipped with the knowledge to harness AI in meaningful and efficient ways.

Remember that AI is a tool—one that can help you solve complex problems, enhance productivity, and open up new avenues for creativity. By continuing to explore and refine your skills, you'll be well-prepared for the future of AI, both in your professional and personal life.

Thank you for joining me in this exploration of local AI. I hope the tools, techniques, and concepts you've learned here empower you to create, innovate, and push the boundaries of what's possible with AI.

The future is yours to shape—keep experimenting, learning, and evolving with AI!

Table of Contents